Picture the Past

LIFE IN A
GREEK
TEMPLE

JANE SHUTER

Heinemann
LIBRARY

www.heinemann.co.uk/library
Visit our website to find out more information about
Heinemann Library books.

To order:
☎ Phone 44 (0) 1865 888066
▤ Send a fax to 44 (0) 1865 314091
▯ Visit the Heinemann Bookshop at
www.heinemann.co.uk/library to browse our catalogue and
order online.

First published in Great Britain by
Heinemann Library, Halley Court, Jordan
Hill, Oxford OX2 8EJ, part of Harcourt
Education.
Heinemann is a registered trademark of
Harcourt Education Ltd.

Editors: Nancy Dickmann and
        Sarah Chappelow
Design: Ron Kamen and
        Dave Oakley/Arnos Design
Illustrations: Barry Atkinson
Maps: Jeff Edwards
Picture Researcher: Erica Newbery
        and Elaine Willis
Production Controller: Camilla Smith

Originated by Modern Age
Printed in China by WKT Company Limited

ISBN 0 431 04295 0
09 08 07 06 05
10 9 8 7 6 5 4 3 2 1

British Library Cataloguing in Publication
Data
Shuter, Jane
Life in a Greek temple. - (Picture the past)
292.3'5
A full catalogue record for this book is
available from the British Library.

Acknowledgements:
The publishers would like to thank the
following for permission to reproduce
photographs: AAAC pp. **10**, **27**; Art
Archive pp. **12**, **17** (Dagli Orti), **20** (Orti),
23 (Orti); Bridgeman p. **24**; British Museum
p. **28**; Corbis pp. **6** (David Lees), **7**, **16**
(Mimo Jodice); Paul Shuter pp. **8**, **15**;
Richard Butcher & Magnet Harlequin pp.
13, **22**; Scala p. **18**; Werner Forman pp.
14, **26**.

Cover photograph of a vase showing an
ancient Greek temple and gods
reproduced with permission of Corbis.

Every effort has been made to contact
copyright holders of any material
reproduced in this book. Any omissions will
be rectified in subsequent printings if
notice is given to the publishers.

Contents

Any words appearing in bold, **like this**, are explained in the Glossary.

Who were the ancient Greeks?

The ancient Greeks lived in many separate **city states**. Each was run in different ways. Sometimes, the city states fought each other. But they shared the same **religion** and language. Religion was important to all ancient Greeks. They believed in many different gods and goddesses, who could affect life on earth. The gods and goddesses had to be **worshipped** to keep them happy. As part of this worship, the ancient Greeks built beautiful **temples** as homes for the gods.

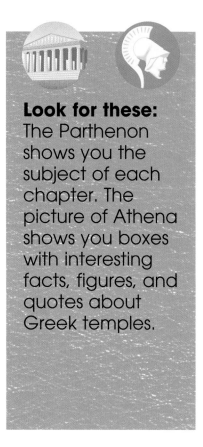

Look for these:
The Parthenon shows you the subject of each chapter. The picture of Athena shows you boxes with interesting facts, figures, and quotes about Greek temples.

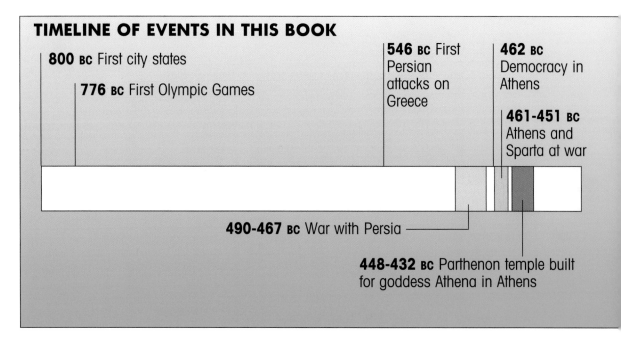

TIMELINE OF EVENTS IN THIS BOOK

800 BC First city states

776 BC First Olympic Games

546 BC First Persian attacks on Greece

462 BC Democracy in Athens

461-451 BC Athens and Sparta at war

490-467 BC War with Persia

448-432 BC Parthenon temple built for goddess Athena in Athens

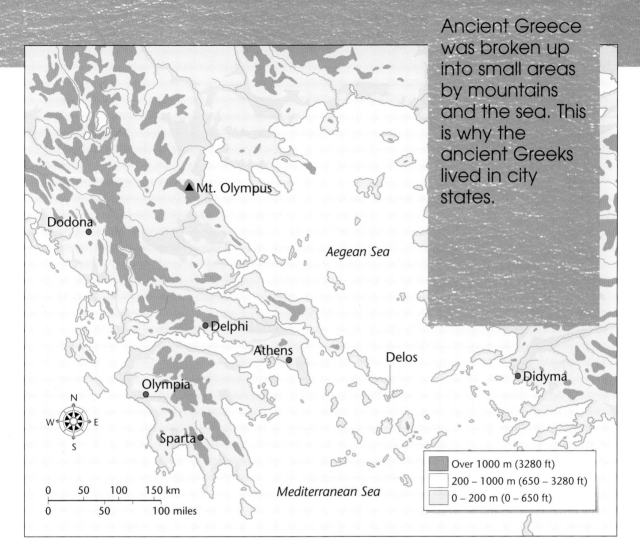

Ancient Greece was broken up into small areas by mountains and the sea. This is why the ancient Greeks lived in city states.

Mt. Olympus

Dodona

Aegean Sea

Delphi

Athens

Delos

Didyma

Olympia

Sparta

N
W   E
S

0   50   100   150 km
0   50   100 miles

Mediterranean Sea

Over 1000 m (3280 ft)
200 – 1000 m (650 – 3280 ft)
0 – 200 m (0 – 650 ft)

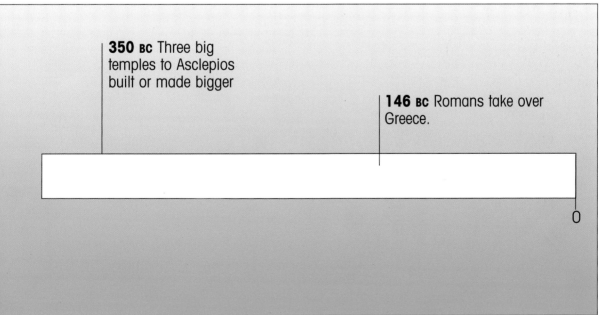

350 BC Three big temples to Asclepios built or made bigger

146 BC Romans take over Greece.

0

Gods and goddesses

We know a lot about the gods and goddesses of ancient Greece because the Greeks told many stories, called **myths**, about them. These stories have been passed down for thousands of years. They are still told today. The most important gods and goddesses were seen as one big family. The ancient Greeks believed that these gods lived on Mount Olympus, a real Greek mountain. This is why the Olympic Games were held nearby, to please Zeus.

WHAT DID THEY CONTROL?

The most important gods and goddesses were thought to be responsible for these things:

Zeus	everything
Hera	marriage
Hades	the dead
Poseidon	the sea
Demeter	farming
Aphrodite	love
Athena	wisdom and war
Apollo	seeing the future
Artemis	hunting
Ares	war
Persephone	the dead
Hephaestus	metalwork
Dionysus	wine
Hermes	travellers and shepherds

The ancient Greeks made many carvings of the gods and goddesses. This one shows Poseidon, Athena, Apollo, and Artemis.

Just like an ordinary Greek family, the gods and goddesses squabbled and made up. In the Greek myths, it was not unusual for the gods to take sides in wars and battles. They did not always support the same side, either. Each **city state** had **temples** to many of the gods and goddesses. But they all chose one god or goddess to take special care of their city state.

This carving shows Athena, goddess of the city state of Athens. She is wearing a helmet and carrying a spear. The sculptor wanted to show her as a goddess of war.

How temples were built

Temples were built as homes for the gods. The ancient Greeks believed their gods lived forever, so needed their temple to last forever. Temples were built from stone or marble, not mud brick like ordinary homes. Temples were built in cities. The most important of them were on the **acropolis**. This was the highest, most defended part of the city. Rich **citizens** of the city sometimes paid for temples to be built. Sometimes they were built by **taxes** paid by all citizens.

When we look at Greek temples now, all we see is the bare stone or marble. But temples were painted all over, inside and out. You can still see the traces of ancient paint on this carving from a temple in Athens.

Temples were made from heavy marble or stone. This was cut into shape at the **quarries** where it was dug out of the ground. It had to be taken to the temple site on carts pulled by oxen. Then it was lifted carefully into place. The ancient Greeks had several ways of doing this, using wooden frames and ropes and **pulleys**.

Temples were decorated beautifully, inside and out. The marble or stone was carved, polished, and painted. Parts of the painting were sometimes done with gold. This was very expensive, so was not done in every temple. Temples faced east, where the sun rose. This was so the statue of the god or goddess could 'see' the **sacrifices** through the door of the **shrine** where the statue stood.

This photo was taken from where sacrifices were held outside a temple on the **acropolis** at Athens. The shrine was right at the back, through two doorways.

The Parthenon is one of the most famous Greek temples. The temple was built just to hold a statue as a gift to Athena. The statue was one of the most expensive ever made. It cost about 5,000,000 **drachmae**. A builder earned about 1 drachma a day.

JUST ONE STATUE

The statue of Athena in the Parthenon, Athens, was made by a famous sculptor called Phidias. He made a wooden frame exactly the right size and shape. Then he made the arms, neck and face out of pieces of ivory. Her eyes were made of jewels and her dress, helmet, and shield were made of gold.

The original statue of Athena did not survive. Copies like this one show us what it would have looked like.

Priests and priestesses

Ordinary **citizens** did not go into most **temples**. Only **priests** and **priestesses**, who served the gods, went inside. There were many kinds of priests and priestesses. High priests were the most important, and ran the temple. They looked after the gifts given to the gods and organized **religious ceremonies**. Usually, priests worked at temples for the male gods. Priestesses worked at temples for the female goddesses.

This vase painting shows priestesses making a **sacrifice**. Sacrifices were the most usual kind of **worship**. Citizens worshipped together and, if the sacrifice was an animal, shared the meat afterwards at a feast.

Priests and priestesses usually came from rich families. Unless they had a very important job in a busy temple, they did not work at the temple all the time. They lived at home and did other things as well. This was another way that religion was part of daily life.

Priests and priestesses wore everyday clothes, although for some festivals they might wear special colours, or a special headdress.

13

Working in a temple

The more important the **temple** was, the more work a **priest** or **priestess** had to do there. There were no daily ceremonies. The statue of the god or goddess was not cleaned and fed each day, as in the ancient Egyptian religion. But people could come to leave **offerings** or ask a favour of the god at any time. So there needed to be at least one priest or priestess in the temple most of the time to deal with these.

OFFERINGS

Offerings were gifts for the gods. People left them when they were asking the gods a favour. They also left them as a thank you if the gods had helped them. They left the most expensive offering they could afford.

This stalk of wheat is made from solid gold. It was an offering made to Demeter, the goddess of farming.

Priests and priestesses ran the **religious festivals**. They organized the processions, played the music, sang the hymns, and made the **sacrifices**. The most important festivals, such as the Olympic Games, were not just for one **city state**. People came to them from all over Greece. This needed a lot of organizing. All the city states had to be told when the festival was going to happen and the different events had to run smoothly.

In this carving, a boy is taking a ram to be sacrificed. Taking part in **religious ceremonies** was an important part of growing up.

Ordinary people **worshipped** the gods at **religious ceremonies** and festivals. But because they believed that the gods could come to earth and affect their daily lives, they also had ceremonies to the gods built into their daily routine. Most homes had statues of Zeus and Apollo in the courtyard, with an **altar** to leave them **offerings**. They prayed at the statue at any time of day or night.

HERMES

Hermes was the messenger of the gods. He was seen as the god of roads, journeys, and trade. Most homes had a carving of Hermes, called a herm, by the front door. This was to take care of people in their daily journeys from home.

This small **terracotta** statue shows the goddess Athena. Terracotta statues were left as gifts for the gods, or buried with a dead person.

All the important times in the lives of the ancient Greeks – births, marriages, and deaths – had religious ceremonies. They did not always need a **priest** or **priestess**. Ordinary people could also perform them. There were also different ceremonies for when children became adults, depending on the **city state** they lived in. In most places, a girl offered her childhood toys to the goddess Artemis on the day before her wedding.

Ordinary people often gave simple offerings to the gods, such as these clay heads.

Festivals

There were many different **religious festivals**, all through the year. The most important of them lasted for several days. These festivals included **sacrifices** and athletic competitions or several plays at the theatre. People took time off work to go to them.

PEACE FOR FESTIVALS

Even fighting stopped for the most important festivals. In 421BC, all the city states fighting in the war between Athens and Sparta agreed, "Anyone who wishes to worship at the temples, make sacrifices, travel to them, and attend the festival are promised that they can travel safely, by land or sea."

These priestesses are taking part in a festival to worship the god Dionysus.

Festivals always had a procession to a **temple**, where animals were killed as sacrifices. Everyone stopped work and watched the procession and shared in the feast after the sacrifice.

Priests usually performed the sacrifices and prayed to the gods at festivals. Priestesses usually played music and danced.

Food and drink

The ancient Greeks ate a lot of fresh fruit and vegetables. They ate cheese and fish regularly, too. Everyone drank wine, even the children, although the wine was watered down. Meat was mainly eaten at **religious festivals**. Rich people also ate meat at other times, on special occasions, such as weddings.

This vase painting shows a priest about to cut up joints of meat after a sacrifice.

Kebabs

Everyone at a festival shared the meat of animals that were killed as **sacrifices**. The easiest way of doing this was to cut it up into small pieces and cook it on sticks – often sticks of the herb rosemary, to add to the flavour.

WARNING: do not cook anything unless there is an adult to help you. Make sure the meat is thoroughly cooked before you eat it.

1 Put the sticks to soak in cold water so they do not burn during cooking. You only need to soak them for a few minutes.

2 Cut the meat into cubes. Put them in a bowl with some oil. Stir to coat all the pieces of meat in oil.

3 Thread the pieces of meat onto the skewers. Do not squash them together, or they will not cook evenly.

4 Sprinkle with the salt and fresh rosemary.

5 Cook under the grill, turning frequently, until the meat is no longer pink inside.

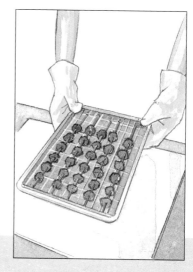

Theatres

The ancient Greeks put on plays as part of **religious festivals**. The most important was the festival of Dionysus, held in March. This festival lasted five days. There were three days of plays, more than one each day. There were always three tragedies and five comedies. The plays were put on in specially built theatres, to entertain the gods and goddesses.

TRAGEDY AND COMEDY

Tragedies were plays where things turned out badly. Often, people in them disobeyed the gods or acted in ways the gods disapproved of. Comedies were often about misunderstandings between humans. They often ended with a wedding, or had slaves in them who fooled about to make the audience laugh.

Theatres were built of stone and were big. They had no shade, unless a person brought a hat or sunshade with them.

The ancient Greeks believed that going to see plays was part of how the gods should be **worshipped**. They believed that the gods would be pleased with them for going. We know that men went to the theatre. We do not know if women went. If they did, they sat in a different part of the theatre to the men. Theatres had no roofs. Even in March, it would have been very hot.

The Olympic Games

The Olympic Games were part of the **religious festival** for the god Zeus, held at Olympia. The festival was held every four years and lasted for five days. Women had their own games, at the same time, in a different part of Olympia. These games were to worship Zeus' wife, Hera. Women could not watch the men's games. People from all over Greece went to the festival, to watch and to take part.

A MARVELLOUS SPECTACLE

During the Olympic Games, there were **sacrifices** and **religious ceremonies**. But the most important part of the festival was the athletic competitions. One Greek writer said, "Aren't you burned by the sun and packed tight together? Aren't you soaked to the skin when it rains? But you put up with it for the marvellous spectacle."

Ancient Greek athletes competed naked. This athlete is throwing a javelin as far as he can.

The only prize for a winner at the Olympic Games was a crown of olive leaves. But the competition to win was fierce and **city states** gave their own prizes to athletes who won at the Olympics. These prizes ranged from free meals to a payment of money every year for the rest of the athletes' lives.

Fitness was very important in ancient Greece. Men from all the city states exercised regularly at the gymnasium – this kept them fit for war.

Oracles

The ancient Greeks went to **temples** to ask the gods for favours. To ask a god questions they went to a **shrine**, called an oracle. They asked the **priest** or **priestess** of the oracle their question. The god or goddess was supposed to answer the question through the priest. Unlike being a temple priest, working at an oracle was a full-time job. The priest or priestess had to actually live in the holy place where the oracle was.

WHERE WERE THEY?

The most famous oracles were at Delphi, Delos, Dodona, and Didyma (see the map on page 5). There were also sacred sites, like a cave at Trophonios, where a person could go to hear the gods answer their question.

This photo shows the Oracle at Delphi today.

A journey to an oracle could take a long time. When the ancient Greeks wanted a less expensive, quicker answer, they asked fortune tellers or **seers**. Both were said to be able to see the future. People would also follow local superstitions. There were many of these and almost anything would do. So birds flying from left to right, a bad storm, or even the number of times a dog barks had special meaning.

Some seers became famous for their fortune telling. This is a statue of the seer Iamos carved on a temple to Zeus. Iamos was the first seer in his family, but his sons and grandsons were also seers.

Special temples

When the ancient Greeks wanted help with their health, they went to an asclepion. This was a **temple** for the god Asclepius, the god of healing. People prayed at the temple and made **offerings**. They swam and washed in the sea, to clean themselves. Then they slept in the temple. This was very unlike other temples, which ordinary people were not allowed in to. **Priests** treated them with ointments and **herbal cures** too.

Grateful people left offerings at the Asclepion. Usually, these offerings showed the part of the body that had been healed.

Patients slept in a special part of the temple, called the abaton. This was a long thin building, open to the air on both sides. The dreams they had while they slept there were said to be messages from Asclepius. They had to tell their dreams to the priests, who worked out what they meant.

Many patients at the asclepion woke the next day, saying they were cured. Others stayed for several days. If the abaton was full, some people slept in nearby courtyards, just to be close to the temple.

Glossary

acropolis hilltop fortress. The most famous are now in Athens.

altar place where offerings were made to gods and goddesses

citizen man who is born in a city to parents who were citizens

city state a city and the land it controls around it

drachmae money used in ancient Greece (and in modern Greece until 2002)

festival see religious festival

herbal cures medicines made from plants

myths stories about the gods

offerings things left in a special place as a present to the gods

priest (priestess) a man (woman) who works in a temple serving a god or goddess

pulleys pieces of wood with grooves for ropes to run in

quarries places where a lot of rock is dug out to make buildings

religion beliefs shared by many people that include believing in one or more gods

religious ceremonies special times when people go to one place to pray to a god or goddess

religious festivals several days of religious ceremonies, held each year

sacrifices something given to a god or a goddess as a gift. Live sacrifices, like animals, were killed before they were given.

seers people who are said to be able to see the future

shrine a holy place

taxes money that you have to pay to the people who run the country you are living in

temple place where gods and goddesses are worshipped

terracotta clay soil and water mixture that is shaped and baked hard to make bowls, cups, or ornaments

worship when a god or goddess is praised or shown respect

Further resources

Books

Ancient Greece, Christine Hatt (Heinemann Library, 2004)
Explore History: Ancient Greece (Heinemann Library, 2001)
History in Art: Ancient Greece, Andrew Langley (Raintree, 2004)
The Ancient Greeks, Pat Taylor (Heinemann Library, 1994)
What families were like: Ancient Greece, Alison Cooper
(Hodder Wayland, 2001)
Worldwise: Ancient Greeks, Daisy Kerr (Franklin Watts, 1997)
You are in Ancient Greece, Ivan Minnis (Raintree, 2004)

Websites

www.ancientgreece.com
A good website looking at all aspects of ancient Greek life.

www.historyforkids.org/learn/greeks
A useful website full of links and extra resources.

www.bbc.co.uk/schools/ancientgreece/main_menu.shtml
Use the games and interactive activities to find out more
about life in ancient Greece.

www.olympic.org/uk/games/ancient/index_uk.asp
Visit this website to find out all about the Olympics.

Disclaimer

All the Internet addresses (URLs) given in this book were valid at the time of going to
press. However, due to the dynamic nature of the Internet, some addresses may have
changed, or sites may have ceased to exist since publication. While the author and
publishers regret any inconvenience this may cause readers, no responsibility for any
such changes can be accepted by either the author or the publishers.

Index

Titles in the *Picture the Past* series include:

Hardback 0431042942

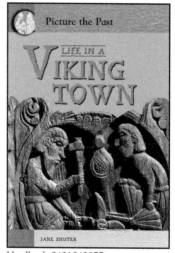

Hardback 0431042977

Hardback 0431042950

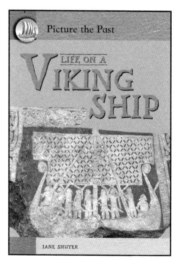

Hardback 0431042985

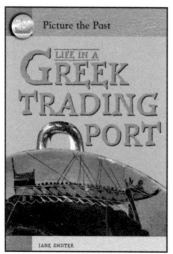

Hardback 0431042969

Find out about the other titles in this series on our website www.heinemann.co.uk/library